DISCOVERING AMERICA

The West

ARIZONA • NEVADA • UTAH

By
Thomas G. Aylesworth
Virginia L. Aylesworth

CHELSEA HOUSE PUBLISHERS
New York • Philadelphia

3   5   7   9   8   6   4   2

Library of Congress Cataloging-in-Publication Data

Aylesworth, Thomas G.
    The West: Arizona, Nevada, Utah
Thomas G. Aylesworth, Virginia L. Aylesworth.
        p. cm.—(Discovering America)
    ISBN 0-7910-3408-9.
        0-7910-3426-7 (pbk.)
        1. Southwest, New—Juvenile literature. 2. Arizona—Juvenile literature. 3. Nevada—Juvenile
literature. 4. Utah—Juvenile literature. [1. Arizona. 2. Nevada. 3. Utah. 4. Southwest, New.]
I. Aylesworth, Virginia L. II. Title. III. Series: Aylesworth, Thomas G. Discovering America.

F787.A96   1995   94-42008
917.9—dc20   CIP
                                        AC

CONTENTS

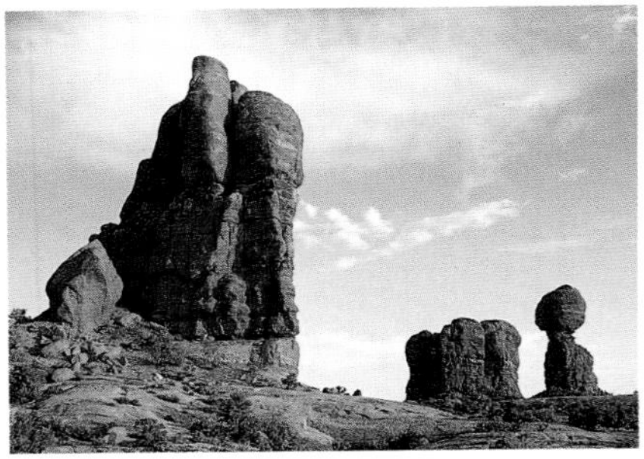

Arizona

The state seal of Arizona, adopted in 1910, is circular. In the center is a shield on which are pictured a miner standing in the mountains; fields; and a cow. These represent the state's minerals industry and agriculture. In the background are mountains, with the sun rising behind them. There is also a storage reservoir, a quartz mill, and a dam. Over all of this is the state motto, and around the edge is printed "Great Seal of the State of Arizona" and "1912," the year of the state's entry into the Union.

ARIZONA
At a Glance

State Flag

Capital: Phoenix

Major Crops: Cotton, sorghum, barley, corn, wheat, citrus fruits

Major Industries: Electronics, mining, agriculture

State Bird: Cactus Wren

State Flower: Saguaro Cactus Blossom

Size: 114,000 square miles (6th largest)
Population: 3,832,294 (23rd largest)

State Flag
The state flag was adopted in 1917. The lower half consists of a solid blue band. In the center is a copper-colored star, and radiating from the star upward are six yellow rays alternating with seven red rays. The star represents the state's chief mineral product, copper. The rays of the setting sun represent the state's location in the west.

State Motto
Ditat Deus
This Latin phrase means "God enriches," and it was selected in 1864.

The Grand Canyon, made a national park in 1919, attracts over 3 million visitors a year.

State Capital

Phoenix has been the capital of Arizona since 1889, long before statehood.

State Name and Nicknames

The Spanish gave Arizona its name in 1736. They took it from two words in the Papago Indian dialect, *Aleh-zon*, which means "little spring." Actually, the spring referred to is now in Mexico.

The most common nickname for Arizona is the *Grand Canyon State*. It is also known as the *Copper State* for its mining, and the *Apache State* for the Indians who once lived there.

The red bloom of the saguaro cactus is the state flower.

State Flower

The bloom of the giant saguaro cactus, *Carnagiea gigantea*, has been the state flower since 1931.

State Tree

Adopted in 1954, the state tree of Arizona is the paloverde, *Cercidium torreyanum*.

State Bird

The cactus wren, *Heleodytes brunneicapillus*, was chosen the state bird in 1931.

State Gem

In 1974, turquoise was picked as the state gem.

State Neckwear

The bola tie was named the state neckwear in 1973.

State Song

The state song of Arizona is "Arizona March Song," with words by Margaret Rowe Clifford and music by Maurice Blumenthal.

Population

The population of Arizona in 1992 was 3,832,294, making it the 23rd most populous state. There are 33.7 people per square mile.

Industries

The principal industries of Arizona are tourism, manufacturing, mining, lumbering, and agriculture. In 1992, tourists spent $7.2 billion in Arizona. The chief manufactured products are electronics, printing and publishing, foods, primary and fabricated metals, aircraft and missiles, and apparel.

Agriculture

The chief crops of the state are cotton, sorghum, barley, corn, wheat, sugar beets, and citrus fruits. Arizona is also a livestock state, and there are estimated to be some 900,000 cattle, 100,000 hogs and pigs, 225,000 sheep, and 325,000 poultry on its farms. Pine fir, and spruce trees are harvested. Copper,

A dramatic view of the Sonoran Desert.

of Representatives. The state has eight votes in the electoral college.

Sports

Arizona is a sports state and a real hotbed of collegiate baseball. The NCAA championship in that sport has been won by Arizona State University (1965, 1967, 1969, 1977, 1981) and the University of Arizona (1976, 1980, 1986). In football, Arizona State won the Rose Bowl in 1987.

On the professional level, the Phoenix Suns of the National Basketball

Two participants in the Loggers' Festival at Payson, Arizona. Timber is one of the state's important agricultural products.

molybdenum, gold, and silver are important mineral resources.

Government

The governor of Arizona is elected to a four-year term, as are the secretary of state, attorney general, state treasurer, and superintendent of public instruction. The state legislature, which meets annually, consists of a 30-member senate and a 60-member house of representatives. All the members serve two-year terms. Each of the 30 legislative districts elects one senator and two representatives for two-year terms. The most recent state constitution was adopted in 1910. In addition to its two U.S. senators, Arizona has six representatives in the House

Football fans in Arizona have the choice of cheering either the college team of Arizona State University or of the University of Arizona, or the NFL Phoenix Cardinals.

Association play in the Arizona Veterans' Memorial Coliseum, and the Phoenix Cardinals of the National Football League play in Sun Devil Stadium in Tempe.

Major Cities

Mesa (population 288,104). Founded in 1878, it was named Mesa—Spanish for "tabletop"—because it lies atop a plateau. The town is one of Arizona's fastest-growing communities; the population of the Phoenix-Mesa area has increased by 39.9 percent between 1980 and 1990.

Things to see in Mesa: Mormon Temple Visitors' Center, Mesa Southwest Museum, Arizona Museum for Youth, Champlin Fighter Museum, Rockin' R Ranch, and Lost Dutchman State Park.

Phoenix (population 983,392). Settled in 1864, the capital city has a glorious climate that attracts many tourists and retirees. This area was first inhabited by the prehistoric Hohakam Indians, a tribe which disappeared by 1450. Englishman "Lord Darrell" Duppa visited this site in 1867 and named it Phoenix, predicting that a city would rise, like the phoenix of legend, from the ruins of the Indian settlement. The most populous city in the state, the population has increased rapidly in the last half of the 20th century, growing 28.6 percent between 1980 and 1990. The Phoenix-Mesa area grew 39.9 percent between 1980 and 1990. Phoenix is the ninth largest city in the United States. Surrounded by mountains

and green irrigated fields, it is a popular resort and retirement spot in addition to being an industrial and agricultural center.

Things to see in Phoenix: Arizona State Capitol Museum, Arizona Museum, Heard Museum of Anthropology and Primitive Art, Arizona Hall of Fame Museum, Desert

The variety and beauty of desert flora is displayed at the Desert Botanical Garden in Phoenix, Arizona.

Old Tucson was built in 1939 as the set for the movie Arizona *at a cost of $250,000.*

The Mystery Castle, built by Boyce Luther Gulley as a "live-in sandcastle" for his daughter, is made of native stone and is located near Phoenix.

Botanical Garden, Phoenix Zoo, Hall of Flame, Pueblo Grande Museum, Phoenix Art Museum, Arizona Mineral Museum, Encanto Park, Arizona History Room, Arizona Historical Society Museum, Arizona Museum of Science and Technology, Bayless Country Store Museum, Heritage Square, Mystery Castle, and Phoenix Mountain Preserve.

Tucson (population 405,371). Founded in 1775, Tucson has existed under four flags: Spain, Mexico, the Confederate States of America, and the United States of America. Today it is a center for health care, tourism, education, mining, and aircraft production.

Things to see in Tucson: Mission San Xavier del Bac, Arizona State Museum, Museum of Art and Faculty of Fine Arts, Mineralogical Museum, Grace H. Flandrau Planetarium, Center for Creative Photography, Arizona Historical Society Museum, Arizona Historical Society Frémont House Museum, Tucson Museum of Art, Arizona Historical Society Fort Lowell Museum, Pima Air Museum, Old Town

Artisans, Tucson Botanical Gardens, Old Pueblo Museum, International Wildlife Museum, Tohono Chul Park, Arizona-Sonora Desert Museum, Old Tucson, and Colossal Cave.

Places to Visit

The National Park Service maintains 28 areas in the state of Arizona: Grand Canyon National Park, Petrified Forest National Park, Canyon de Chelly National Monument, Casa Grande National Monument, Chiricahua National Monument, Montezuma Castle National Monument, Navajo National Monument, Organ Pipe Cactus National Monument, Pipe Spring National Monument, Saguaro National Monument, Sunset Crater National Monument, Tumacacori National Monument, Wupatki National Monument, Tonto National Monument, Tuzigoot National Monument, Walnut Canyon National Monument, Hohokam Pima National

Visitors touring the Queen Mine in Bisbee. Copper was first discovered there in 1875 by a prospector who was actually looking for silver or gold.

Monument, Coronado National Memorial, Glen Canyon Recreation Area, Lake Mead National Recreation Area, Hubbell Trading Post Historic Site, Fort Bowie National Historic Site, Apache-Sitgreaves National Forest, Coconino National Forest, Coronado National Memorial Forest, Kaibab Indian Preservation, Prescott National Forest, and Tonto National Monument.

In addition, there are 12 state recreation areas.

Bisbee: Queen Mine Tour. Visitors may take a one-and-a-half-hour guided tour on a copper mine train.

Camp Verde: Fort Verde State Historical Park. Four original buildings remain of this Indian Wars fort.

Chandler: Gila Bend Indian Reservation. More than 30 Indian tribes are represented in this artist and artisan center.

Flagstaff: Lowell Observatory. It was from here that the planet

Pluto was discovered in 1930.
Gila Bend: Painted Rocks State Park. Ancient Indian rock paintings can be seen here.
Globe: Besh-Ba-Gowah Indian Ruins. These ruins of a Salado Indian village date back more than 700 years.
Jerome: This is an old copper-mining town with cobblestone streets.
Kingman: Bonelli House. Built in 1894, this building has been restored and contains many original pieces.
Lake Havasu City: London Bridge English Village. This 21-acre village features the original London Bridge.
Litchfield Park: Wildlife World Zoo. The zoo houses exotic

London Bridge, built in 1831, was purchased by Robert McCulloch and relocated to Lake Havasu City in 1971. It connects an island in the lake with the mainland.

animals and a children's petting zoo.

Nogales: Tubac Presidio State Historical Park. The ruins of Arizona's first European settlement, built in 1752, can be seen here.

Patagonia: Stradling Museum of the Horse. Exhibits tell the story of the horse from ancient Greek times.

Prescott: Sharlot Hall Museum. This contains the old governor's mansion (1864) and other structures.

Scottsdale: Taliesin West. This is the winter campus of the Frank Lloyd Wright Foundation.

Sedona: Tlaquepaque. Art galleries and stores are located in a Spanish-style courtyard.

Sierra Vista: Fort Huachuca. The "old post" area dates back to 1885.

Superior: Boyce Thompson Southwestern Arboretum. Semi-desert plants from around the world can be seen on this 420-acre tract.

Tempe: Niels Petersen House. This Victorian home was built in 1892.

Tombstone: Bird Cage Theatre. This frontier cabaret was built in the 1880s.

Wickenburg: Frontier Street. The street has been preserved as it was in the early 1900s.

Sharlot Hall Museum in Prescott, Arizona, served as the territorial capitol from 1863 to 1867, and from 1877 to 1889.

The Tlaquepaque courtyard is home to a number of galleries and boutiques.

Window Rock: Navajo Tribal Museum. Exhibits show Navajo history, art, and culture.

Winslow: Meteor Crater. The world's best-preserved meteorite crater measures 4,150 feet from rim to rim.

Yuma: Yuma Territorial Prison State Historic Park. The ruins of the 1876 prison can be seen here.

Events

There are many events and organizations that schedule activities of various kinds in the state of Arizona. Here are some of them:

Sports: La Vuelta de Bisbee (Bisbee), Fiesta Days (Carefree), Horse races (Douglas), Cochise County Fair and College Rodeo (Douglas), Junior Parade (Florence), Thunderbird Balloon Classic 100 Hot-Air Balloon Race and Air Show (Glendale), Copper Dust Stampede Days (Globe), Navajo County Horse Races (Greer), Chili Cook-Off (Kingman), Havasu Classic Outboard World Championships (Lake Havasu City), Parker-Score 400 Off Road Race (Parker), Enduro Boat Race (Parker), All-Indian Rodeo (Parker), Sawdust Festival, Loggers' Competition (Payson), World's Oldest Continuous PRCA Rodeo (Payson), Aid to Zoo National Horse Show (Phoenix), LPGA Samaritan Turquoise Classic (Phoenix), National Hot Rod Association Drag Racing (Phoenix), Phoenix Formula I Grand Prix (Phoenix), World's Championship Jaycees Rodeo of Rodeos (Phoenix), Prescott Frontier Days Rodeo (Prescott), Parada del Sol and Rodeo (Scottsdale), Rodeo (Show Low), Fiesta Bowl Football Classic (Tempe), La Fiesta de los Vaqueros Rodeo (Tucson), Tucson Balloon Festival (Tucson), Tucson Open (Tucson), Rex Allen Days PRCA Rodeo (Willcox), Bill Williams Rendezvous Days (Williams), Cowpunchers' Reunion and Old-Timers' Rodeo (Williams), Powwow and PRCA Rodeo (Window Rock), Thoroughbred and Quarter Horse Racing (Yuma).

Arts and Crafts: Hopi Artists' Exhibition (Flagstaff), Navajo Artists' Exhibition (Flagstaff), Annual Vahki Exhibition (Mesa), Cactus Show (Phoenix), Cowboy Artists of America Exhibition (Phoenix), Gem and Mineral

The A to Z Horse Show is held every January to benefit the Phoenix Zoo.

Cowboys making their grand entrance to the rodeo. The first formal rodeo was held at Prescott, Arizona, in 1888.

Show (Phoenix), George Phippen Memorial Western Art Show (Prescott), Territorial Prescott Days (Prescott), Art in the Park (Sierra Vista), Winter Arts Festival (Sierra Vista), Festival of the Arts (Tubac), Gem and Mineral Show (Tucson), Southwest Antique Guild Show and Sale (Yuma).

Music: Country Music Festival (Flagstaff), Flagstaff Festival of the Arts (Flagstaff), Old-Time Fiddlers Contest (Globe), Square Dance Festival (Globe), Country Music Festival (Payson), Old-Time Fiddlers Contest and Festival (Payson), Arizona Opera Company (Phoenix), Ballet Arizona (Phoenix), Phoenix Symphony (Phoenix), Phoenix Chamber Music Society (Phoenix), Arizona State University Lyric Opera (Phoenix), Phoenix Boys Choir (Phoenix), Valley of the Sun Annual Square and Round Dance Festival (Phoenix), Bluegrass Festival (Prescott), Southern Arizona Light Opera

The boats are the floats in the Lighted Boat Parade held in Parker, Arizona.

Company (Tucson), Tucson Pops Orchestra (Tucson), Arizona Opera Company (Tucson), Southern Arizona Square and Round Dance Festival (Tucson), Tucson Symphony (Tucson), Four Corners States Bluegrass Music Finals (Wickenburg).

Entertainment: Lost Dutchman Days (Apache Junction), Billy Moore Days (Avondale), O'Odham Tash-Casa Grande's Indian Days (Casa Grande), Verde Valley Fair (Cottonwood), Fort Verde Days (Cottonwood), Cinco de Mayo (Douglas), Fiesta Patrias (Douglas), Coconino County Fair (Flagstaff), Gila County Fair (Globe), Billy Moore Days (Goodyear), Navajo County Fair (Greer), Mohave

County Fair (Kingman), London Bridge Days (Lake Havasu City), Mesa Youthfest (Mesa), Cinco de Mayo Fiesta (Nogales), La Paz County Fair (Parker), Holiday Lighted Boat Parade (Parker), Fiesta Bowl Parade (Phoenix), Indian Fair (Phoenix), Maricopa County Fair (Phoenix), National Livestock Show (Phoenix), Yaqui Indian Holy Week Ceremonials (Phoenix), Agricultural Trade Fair (Phoenix), Arizona State Fair (Phoenix), Smoki Ceremonial and Snake Dance (Prescott), Yavapai County Fair (Prescott), Fiesta de Mayo (Safford), Pioneer Days (Safford), Graham County Fair (Safford), All-Arabian Horse Show (Scottsdale), Fiesta del Tlaquepaque (Sedona), Festival of Lights at Tlaquepaque (Sedona), Christmas Parade (Sierra Vista), Coronado Borderlands Festival (Sierra Vista), Springfest (Tempe), Fiesta Bowl Pep Rally (Tempe), Territorial Days (Tombstone), Wyatt Earp Days (Tombstone), Wild West Days and Rendezvous of Gunfighters (Tombstone), "Helldorado" (Tombstone), Oktoberfest (Tucson), Pima County Fair (Tucson), Pioneer Days at Fort Lowell Park (Tucson), Tucson Festival (Tucson), Fiesta del Presidio (Tucson), San Xavier Pageant and Fiesta (Tucson), Yaqui Indian Easter Ceremony (Tucson), Gold

Rush Days (Wickenburg), Navajo Nation Fair (Window Rock), Yuma County Fair (Yuma).

Tours: Paseo de Casas (Cottonwood), Grand Canyon Helicopter Tours (Grand Canyon National Park), Yuma River Tours (Yuma).

Theater: Arizona Theatre Company (Phoenix), The Phoenix Little Theatre (Phoenix), Stagebrush Theater (Phoenix), Celebrity Theatre (Phoenix), Gaslight Theatre (Tucson), The Invisible Theatre (Tucson), Arizona Theatre Company (Tucson).

Petrified Forest National Park.

These and other petroglyphs illustrate the lives and cultures of ancient Indian civilizations.

Horseback riders follow a
scenic trail through the desert
outside Tucson.

The Land and the Climate

Arizona is bounded on the west by Nevada, California, and the
Mexican state of Baja California; on the north by Nevada and Utah;
on the east by New Mexico; and on the south by the Mexican state
of Sonora. There are two main land regions in the state: the
Colorado Plateau and the Basin and Range Region.

The Colorado Plateau is in northern Arizona and covers about
two-fifths of the state. This is a highland with level surfaces broken
by occasional canyons and mountains, including the San Francisco
and White Ranges. Near Flagstaff is Humphreys Peak, 12,670 feet
above sea level, which is the highest point in Arizona. The major
canyons are the famous Grand Canyon of the Colorado, Canyon de
Chelly, and Oak Creek Canyon. Other natural wonders of the area
are the Painted Desert, Monument Valley, and the Petrified Forest.
The plateau is a land of sheep and cattle ranches and of zinc,
uranium, lead, and copper mines.

The Grand Canyon, one of the most awesome spectacles in the world, was carved by erosion and the Colorado River over two billion years.

The Chiricahua National Monument, named for the fierce Indian tribe that lived in the area, is a series of impressive rock formations.

The Basin and Range Region covers the southern part of the state and a narrow strip in the west. The mountain ranges here run from northwest to southeast, and their names evoke Arizona's Indian and Spanish heritage: the Gila, Mazatzal, Chiricahua, Huachuca, Hualpai, Pinaleño, Santa Catalina, and Santa Rita. Broad desert basins lie between the mountains. Most of the region is very dry, but the soil is fertile, and effective use of irrigation makes it possible to raise a variety of crops and livestock. Vegetables, wheat, barley, hay, grapes, sorghum, potatoes, and cotton are cultivated in this area. Cattle ranches abound, and mines in the region yield copper, iron ore, molybdenum, tungsten, gold, silver, zinc, and lead.

The most important river in Arizona is the Colorado, which runs for 688 miles within the state. Many irrigation and electrical-power dams span its waters. Most of the state's other rivers and streams are dry for part of the year. All of Arizona's larger lakes are manmade, many of them created by damming streams.

Rain falls where it is least needed in Arizona, with precipitation averaging 5 inches in the populous south and 30 inches in the remote mountain areas. Because of the range of elevations, temperatures vary greatly from one part of the state to another, although humidity is uniformly low. In southern Arizona, temperatures average 50 degrees Fahrenheit in January and 90 degrees F. in July.

The landscape around Sedona is filled with scrub trees and many varieties of cactus.

Once the home of the Anasazi Indians, Canyon de Chelly, in the northeast corner of Arizona is part of the Navajo reservation. Several Navajo families still live and graze their sheep on the canyon floor.

The History

Before Spanish explorers came to what is now Arizona, people had been living there for thousands of years. Their ways of life, or cultures, are known to us as the Anasazi, the Mogollon, and the Holokam. The Anasazi, who lived in northeastern Arizona for a thousand years, first lived in pithouses but later built spectacular cliff dwellings and made elaborate decorated baskets and pottery. They were the ancestors of the Pueblo Indians.

The people of the Holokam culture lived in the Gila River Valley during the same era as the Anasazi. They were probably the first Southwestern people to build irrigation ditches for their fields. They were the ancestors of the present-day Papago and Pima Indians.

The members of the Mogollon culture lived in the mountains of southeastern Arizona from more than 2000 years ago to A.D. 1300. The Mogollon are considered to be the first farmers in the region. In the early 1500s, nomadic Apache and Navajo tribes moved into the area.

During the early 16th century, Spanish settlers in New Spain (now Mexico) began to hear rumors of the Seven Cities of Cibola—Indian cities that possessed great wealth in the form of gold. Legends begun by Spanish explorers placed the cities in what is now the southwestern United States. The Spaniards began to send out expeditions to the area in search of the gold, which, unfortunately, existed only in their imaginations.

The first Spaniard to set foot in present-day Arizona was probably the Franciscan friar Marcos de Niza, who arrived in the San Pedro Valley in 1539 on his search for the Seven Cities. In 1540 came the Spanish explorer Francisco Vásquez de Coronado, who found Hopi and Zuñi villages, but, of course, no gold.

During the late 1600s, New Spain sent Roman Catholic priests and monks into the region to establish missions. Among them was

Montezuma Castle Natural Monument, a five-story, 20-room cliff dwelling, was built in the 13th century.

The beautiful Mission San Xavier del Bac, built in 1783, is a fine example of Spanish colonial architecture. Its stone facade is elaborately carved.

Eusebio Francisco Kino, a Jesuit missionary who explored and mapped much of present-day Arizona. From 1690 to 1711 he taught the Indians both Christianity and European farming methods, traveling as far north as what is now Fairbank and setting up 24 missions.

Trouble broke out between the nomadic hunting tribes and the Spanish in the early 1700s. The Indians made several attempts to drive out the European invaders, but Spanish troops were always able to regain the territory they had lost. Eventually, the hard-fighting Apache and Navajo were subdued for a time, and in 1752 Spanish troops set up their first permanent garrison in Arizona—a fort at Tubac. It had thick adobe walls, built of sun-dried mud bricks in the Pueblo Indian style. The heat of the desert and the lack of wood for building made this type of shelter predominant for centuries.

When Mexico gained its independence from Spain by revolution in 1821, Arizona became a part of Mexico. During the next few decades, American and French trappers moved in to explore for furs. When the Mexican War broke out between the United States and Mexico in 1846, U.S. forces took control of the Arizona region and most of the Southwest. At the end of the war, in 1848, Mexico ceded more than a million square miles of territory, including what is now Arizona and New Mexico as far south as the Gila River. Many Easterners thought that all they were getting was worthless desert. In 1853 the Gadsden Purchase from Mexico extended the southern boundary to the present-day border with Mexico.

In spite of assertions that the land was useless, American pioneers began moving west into Arizona. Because many of them were from the South, they favored the Confederates when the Civil War broke out in 1861. Arizona sent a delegation to the Confederate Congress, and in 1862 the Confederacy sent troops to occupy both Arizona and New Mexico. However, Union forces defeated the Confederates and ignored their claim to a "Confederate Territory of Arizona." In 1863 the federal government created the Arizona Territory, with boundaries approximately the same as they are now.

The first territorial governor, John N. Goodwin, set up his headquarters at Fort Whipple and lived a few miles from the fort. His home was only a log house, but it was the first governor's mansion, and the town of Prescott grew up around it.

Trouble with the Indians continued, as Arizona tribes resisted being crowded onto reservations and deprived of their ancestral ways of life. The Navajo were defeated in 1863 by U.S. troops led by Kit Carson, the famous scout. But the Chiricahua Apache continued to raid lonely ranches and outposts in the southwest. They also raided towns and forts, under brilliant military leaders like Mangas Coloradas, his son-in-law, Cochise, and Geronimo (born Goyathlay). It wasn't until 1886 that Geronimo finally surrendered to General Nelson A. Miles.

Geronimo (1829–1909) was the chief of the Chiricahua Apache and led his tribe in many raids against the white settlers of New Mexico and Arizona.

Despite the Indian wars, settlers kept coming into Arizona, especially after the discovery of silver, copper, and gold. Irrigation projects helped make the soil productive. Farmers in the Salt River Valley, near what is now Phoenix, were among the first to use irrigation extensively. Large-scale farming and ranching developed, and in 1877 the Southern Pacific Railroad reached Arizona from California.

During this period of growth, Arizona applied for statehood repeatedly. Congress wanted to create a single state from the Arizona and New Mexico Territories, but Arizona resisted, holding out for statehood in its own right. Finally, in 1912, it became the 48th state of the Union. During the next generation, the federal government fostered Arizona's development through water-conservation projects and promotion of the state's many scenic attractions. Copper mining also grew in importance.

World War II brought a major population increase, as air bases and war plants were built in Arizona. Wartime demand stimulated the cattle, copper, and cotton industries. The boom years had begun: Arizona's population grew by 50 percent in the 1940s and by 74 percent in the 1950s. Manufacturing became increasingly important, and thousands of tourists came to see the wonders of the Grand Canyon, the Painted Desert, and the Petrified Forest.

Today Arizona is still home to almost 150,000 Indians—more than half of them Navajo—living on 20 reservations. No other state has as many Indian residents. The Navajo Indians form the largest tribe on the largest U.S. reservation. Arizona is a land of contrasts, where the gleaming high-rise buildings of Phoenix coexist with ancient cliff dwellings and varicolored deserts. In the three decades from 1960 to 1990, the population of Arizona grew by an astounding 250 percent.

The McMath Solar Telescope, one of the largest in the world, is at the Kitt Peak Observatory outside Tucson.

Education

Spanish missionaries established the first schools in Arizona in the late 1600s to teach Christianity to the Indians. After Mexico broke with Spain, however, the Mexican government expelled the religious

Phoenix, the state capital, is a modern sunbelt city with many high-rise apartments and office buildings.

At right:
The influence of nearby Mexico is apparent in the popular fiestas held throughout the state of Arizona.

Below:
Many Apache Indians live on the reservations scattered across the state.

orders. The first public school opened in Tucson in 1871 to meet the educational needs of American settlers. When Arizona became a state in 1912, it had two institutions of higher education, both founded in 1865: the University of Arizona and Arizona State University.

The People

Approximately 79 percent of Arizonans live in metropolitan areas such as Phoenix, Tucson, and Mesa. About 92 percent of them were born in the United States, and 6 percent are Indians. Most of those born in other countries came from Mexico. The Roman Catholic Church is the largest single religious body in the state, and the largest Protestant community is the Church of Jesus Christ of Latter-day Saints (the Mormons). Arizona also has many Baptists, Episcopalians, Methodists, and Presbyterians.

Famous People

Many famous people were born in the state of Arizona. Here are a few:

Rose Elizabeth Bird b. 1936, Tucson. Chief justice of the California supreme court

Cesar Chavez 1927-93, Yuma. Union leader

Cochise 1812-74, Apache leader

Joan Ganz Cooney b. 1929, Phoenix. Founder of Children's TV Workshop, producer of *Sesame Street*

John Denny b. 1952, Prescott. Baseball pitcher

Andy Devine 1905-77, Flagstaff. Cowboy film comedian

Barbara Eden b. 1934, Tucson. Television actress: *I Dream of Jeannie*

Sean Elliott b. 1968, Tucson. Basketball player

Gary Gentry b. 1946, Phoenix. Baseball pitcher

Geronimo 1829-1909, Apache leader

Barry Goldwater b. 1909, Phoenix. Senate leader and presidential candidate

Billy Hatcher b. 1960, Williams. Baseball player

Carl Hayden 1877-1972, Tempe. Senate leader

Richard B. Kleindienst b. 1923, near Winslow. U.S. attorney general

Charlie Mingus 1922-79, Nogales. Jazz bassist

Sandra Day O'Connor b. 1930, near Duncan. U.S. Supreme Court justice

Barry Goldwater, the long-time Senator from Arizona, ran for President on the Republican ticket in 1964.

Morris K. Udall served Arizona as a member of the U.S. House of Representatives for 30 years.

Alexander M. Patch 1889-1945, Fort Huachuca, Arizona Territory. Army officer

Marty Robbins 1925-82, Glendale. Country-and-western singer

Linda Ronstadt b. 1946, Tucson. Pop singer

Paul Silas b. 1943, Prescott. Basketball player

Morris K. Udall b. 1922, St. Johns. Congressman

Stewart L. Udall b. 1920, St. Johns. U.S. secretary of the interior

Colleges and Universities

There are many colleges and universities in Arizona. Here are the more prominent, with their locations, dates of founding, and enrollments.

Arizona State University, Tempe, 1885, 43,635

DeVry Institute of Technology, Phoenix, 1967, 2,563

Embry-Riddle Aeronautical University, Prescott, 1978, 1,661

Grand Canyon College, Phoenix, 1949, 1,747

Northern Arizona University, Flagstaff, 1899, 18,491

University of Arizona, Tucson, 1885, 35,129

University of Phoenix, Phoenix, 1976, 7,700

Western International University, Phoenix, 1978, 1,552

Where To Get More Information

Arizona Office of Tourism
1100 West Washington
Phoenix, AZ 85007
Or call 1-602-542-3618

Nevada

The state seal of Nevada, adopted in 1866, is circular. On it are depicted a plow and sheaf of wheat (representing agriculture) and a quartz mill, mine tunnel, and carload of ore (standing for mineral wealth). In the middle distance are a railroad train and telegraph lines. In the background, the sun rises behind a range of snow-capped mountains. Around the drawing are 36 stars (Nevada is the 36th state) and the state motto. Around the outside of the seal is printed "The Great Seal of the State of Nevada."

NEVADA
At a Glance

Capital: Carson City

Major Industries: Electronics, chemicals, tourism
Major Crops: Alfalfa, potatoes, hay, barley, wheat, cotton

State Bird:
Mountain Bluebird

State Flower:
Sagebrush

Size: 110,561 square miles (7th largest)
Population: 1,327,387 (38th largest)

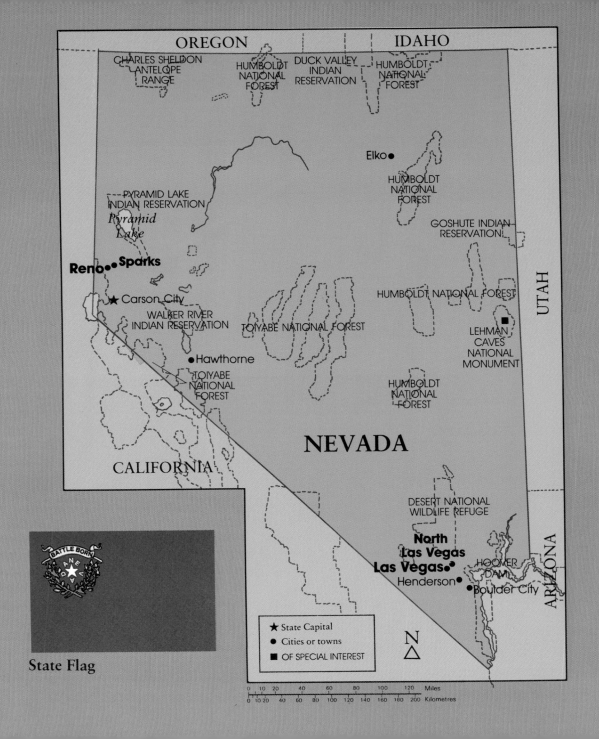

OREGON IDAHO

CHARLES SHELDON
ANTELOPE
RANGE

HUMBOLDT
NATIONAL
FOREST

DUCK VALLEY
INDIAN
RESERVATION

HUMBOLDT
NATIONAL
FOREST

Elko●

HUMBOLDT
NATIONAL
FOREST

PYRAMID LAKE
INDIAN RESERVATION

GOSHUTE INDIAN
RESERVATION

Pyramid
Lake

Reno●● Sparks

UTAH

HUMBOLDT NATIONAL FOREST

★ Carson City

WALKER RIVER
INDIAN RESERVATION

TOIYABE NATIONAL FOREST

LEHMAN
CAVES
NATIONAL
MONUMENT

● Hawthorne

TOIYABE
NATIONAL
FOREST

HUMBOLDT
NATIONAL
FOREST

NEVADA

CALIFORNIA

DESERT NATIONAL
WILDLIFE REFUGE

**North
Las Vegas**
Las Vegas●

HOOVER
DAM

Henderson ●

● Boulder City

ARIZONA

★ State Capital
● Cities or towns
■ OF SPECIAL INTEREST

N
△

0 10 20   40   60   80   100   120   Miles
0 10 20 40 60 80 100 120 160 180 200 Kilometres

State Flag

State Flag

The current state flag was adopted in 1929. It is blue, and in the upper corner nearest the staff is a silver star, under which are two crossed sprays of sagebrush. The letter *N* is located above the top point of the star, and the letters *E, V, A, D,* and *A* are located between the points. Above all this is the phrase "Battle Born," signifying the fact that Nevada was made a state during the Civil War.

State Motto

All For Our Country

This patriotic motto was selected in 1866.

The Snake Mountain Range in Nevada.

State Capital

Carson City has been the state capital since the creation of the Nevada Territory in 1861.

State Name and Nicknames

The name Nevada was given to the region by seventeenth- and eighteenth-century Spanish sailors who were sailing between the Philippines and Mexico. They saw California mountain ranges from far out at sea and called them "Sierra Nevada," or "snowy range." When the Nevada Territory was created, it was first thought that it ought to be called Sierra Nevada, but this was quickly shortened to Nevada.

Nevada has several nicknames. It is called the *Silver State* and the *Mining State* for its silver mines. It is also called the *Sage State* and the *Sagebrush State* for the wild sage that grows there, and the *Battle Born State* because it entered the Union during the Civil War.

State Flower

The sagebrush, *Artemisia tridentata,* was adopted as state flower in 1967. It had been the unofficial state blossom since 1917.

State Tree

Nevada has two official state trees. The single-leaf piñon, *Pinus monophylla,* was selected as state tree in 1959. In 1987, the bristlecone pine tree, *Pinus aristata,* was also designated state tree by the Nevada legislature.

State Bird

Adopted in 1967, the mountain bluebird, *Sialia currucoides,* is the state bird.

State Animal

The desert bighorn sheep, *Ovis canadensis,* has been the state animal since 1973.

State Rock

Sandstone is the official state rock.

State Colors

Silver and blue were named the colors of Nevada in 1983.

State Fish

The Lohonton cutthroat trout, *Salmo clarki,* was selected as state fish in 1981.

State Fossil

The state fossil, adopted in 1977, is the ichthyosaur, an extinct prehistoric marine reptile.

State Grass

Indian rice grass, *Oryzopsis*

The bristlecone pine is one of the two state trees.

hymenoides, was named the state grass in 1977.

State Metal

Silver was adopted as state metal in 1977.

State Song

In 1933, "Home Means Nevada," words and music by Bertha Raffetto, was named the state song of Nevada.

Population

The population of Nevada in 1992 was 1,327,387, making it the 38th most populous state. There are 20.9 people per square mile.

Industries

The principal industries of Nevada are gambling, gaming, tourism, mining, agriculture, manufacturing, government warehousing, and trucking. In 1991, tourists spent over $10 billion in Nevada. The chief manufactured products are gaming devices, chemicals, aerospace products, lawn and

Bighorn, or Rocky Mountain sheep, are a favorite target of hunters, causing the animal's population to dwindle drastically.

garden irrigation equipment, and seismic and machinery-monitoring devices.

Agriculture

The chief crops of the state are alfalfa seed, potatoes, hay, barley, and wheat. Nevada is also a livestock state. There are estimated to be some 480,000 cattle, 10,000 hogs and pigs, 91,000 sheep, and 12,000 chickens and turkeys on its farms. Piñon, juniper, and other pine trees are

harvested. Gold, silver, barite, and construction sand and gravel are important mineral resources.

Government

The governor of Nevada is elected to a four-year term, as are the lieutenant governor, secretary of state, treasurer, controller, and attorney general. The state legislature, which meets in odd-numbered years, consists of a 21-member senate and a 42-

The Spring Mountains provide a backdrop for this alfalfa field near Pahrump.

member assembly. Senators, who serve four-year terms, are elected from Nevada's 21 senatorial districts. Assemblymen, who serve two-year terms, are elected from 42 assembly districts. Each senatorial and assembly district elects one member. The most recent state constitution was adopted in 1864. In addition to its two U.S. senators, Nevada has two representatives in the House of Representatives. The state has four votes in the electoral college.

Sports

Sports are popular in the state of Nevada. On the collegiate level, the NCAA basketball championship was won by the University of Nevada, Las Vegas, in 1990.

Major Cities

Carson City (population 40,443). Founded in 1858, the capital city is situated near the edge of the eastern slope of the Sierra Nevada. It is a trading center for livestock, farm products, and minerals.

Hoover Dam, the largest dam ever built, manages to tame the mighty Colorado River, which carved out the Grand Canyon.

In addition, Carson City is a resort city with a large and growing tourist business that is attracted by the pleasant weather and the casinos. First called Eagle Ranch, it was renamed for the famous scout Kit Carson.

Things to see in Carson City: State Capitol, State Library Building, Nevada State Museum, Stewart Indian Museum, Warren Engine Company No. 1 Fire Museum, Nevada State Railroad Museum, and Bowers Mansion (1864).

Las Vegas (population 258,204). First settled in 1855 by Mormons, the town was abandoned two years later because it had been unprofitable. In 1864 the U.S. Army established a military post at nearby Fort Baker, and the town began to grow with the arrival of the railroad in 1905. Gambling was legalized in Nevada in 1931 and Las Vegas became a major entertainment center after World War II. The most populous city in Nevada, it is a major tourist center boasting night clubs, casinos, resort hotels, and elaborate theatrical productions. Over 10 million people visit its tree-lined avenues each year. Its dry desert climate has made Las Vegas and its environs a popular retirement area.

Things to see in Las Vegas: The Strip, Convention Center, Liberace Museum, Las Vegas Art Museum, Las Vegas Museum of Natural History, Nevada State Museum and Historical Society, Donna Beam Fine Art Gallery, Old Mormon Fort, Ripley's "Believe It or Not," Imperial Palace Auto Collection, Wet 'n Wild, Spring Mountain Ranch, and Bonnie Springs Old Nevada.

The lights of Las Vegas casinos.

Reno (population 133,850). Founded in 1868, the "Biggest Little City in the World" was first known as Lake's Crossing. Historically an important rail link with Virginia City, today Reno attracts many tourists to its numerous hotels and casinos. Its favorable location in the West and its tax structure have encouraged many firms to build facilities here. It was eventually renamed to honor General Jesse Lee Reno, a Union officer of the Civil War.

Things to see in Reno: Fleischmann Planetarium, Nevada Historical Society Museum, William F. Harrah Foundation National Automobile Museum, Wilbur D. May Museum and Arboretum, Mackay School of Mines Museum, and Sierra Nevada Museum of Art.

Virginia City (population 1,826). Settled in 1859 as a mining camp on the eastern slope of Mt. Davidson, Virginia City thrived during the gold and silver rush and was the sight of balls, grand opera, Broadway hits, and private parties in the mansions on "Millionaire's Row." Trains carried passengers to and from San

Francisco and this route was recorded as the most profitable short line. The population of Virginia City declined when the price of silver fell in 1876. The "world's liveliest ghost town," today Virginia City has as many as 40,000 weekly visitors come to its Victorian lodging houses and atmospheric saloons. Its economy is solely dependent upon tourism.

Places to Visit

The National Park Service maintains five areas in the state of Nevada: Lake Mead National Recreation Area, part of Death Valley National Monument, Great Basin National Park, Humboldt National Forest, and Toiyabe National Forest. In addition, there are 20 state recreation areas.

Austin: Stokes Castle. This three-story stone building can be seen for miles.

Elko: Northeastern Nevada Museum. Exhibits on the area's Indian heritage and mining tradition are featured.

The National Automobile Museum has displays illustrating every development of automotive history.

Ely: Nevada Northern Railway Museum. This museum is housed in the 1906 Nevada Northern Railway depot.

Fallon: Churchill County Museum and Archives. Memorabilia of the Pony Express and Transcontinental Telegraph are displayed.

Genoa: Mormon Station Historic Monument. This restored stockade and trading post was built in 1851.

Henderson: Ethel M. Chocolate Factory and Cactus Garden. Visitors may tour the factory and adjacent gardens, which contain 350 species of desert plants.

Incline Village: Ponderosa Ranch and Western Theme Park. Here is the Cartwright House of the *Bonanza* television series.

Lovelock: Courthouse Park. The only round courthouse still in use is located here.

Overton: Lost City Museum of Archeology. Several Pueblo-type houses and Indian relics dating back 10,000 years are featured.

Sparks: Wild Island. This amusement area contains water rides, a game arcade, and miniature golf.

Tonopah: Mizpah Hotel. Built in 1907, this restored mining hotel is a Victorian building.

Virginia City: The Castle. Built in 1868, this was styled after a castle in Normandy, France.

Winnemucca: Humboldt Museum. Exhibits here feature Indian and pioneer artifacts.

Yerington: Fort Churchill Historic State Monument. This post was garrisoned from 1860 to 1869 as a defense against the Paiute Indians.

Participants race for the finish line in the Bristlecone Chariot Races.

Events

There are many events and organizations that schedule activities of various kinds in the state of Nevada. Here are some of them:

Sports: Lincoln County Fair and Rodeo (Caliente), Whistle-Off (Carson City), Elko Expo Open (Elko), Western Festival (Elko), Bristlecone Birkebeiner Ski Race (Ely), Bristlecone Chariot Races (Ely), Wild Bunch Stampede Rodeo (Fallon), All Indian Rodeo (Fallon), US Bass Lake Mead National Draw Tournament (Lake Mead), Las Vegas Invitational Golf Tournament (Las Vegas), Imperial Palace Antique Auto Run (Las Vegas), Showboat Invitational Bowling Tournament (Las Vegas), World Series of Poker (Las Vegas), National Finals Rodeo (Las Vegas), Nissan/Mint 400 Off-Road Race (Las Vegas), Winter Carnival (Reno), Snafflebit Futurity (Reno), Great Balloon Race (Reno), Reno Rodeo (Reno), National Championship Air Races (Reno), National Championship Camel Races (Virginia City), 100-Mile Horse Endurance Race (Virginia City), Wells Pony Express Race (Wells), Tri-County Fair and Oldest Nevada Rodeo (Winnemucca).

More than 6,000 people convene every year to hear working cowboys recite traditional and original cowboy poetry at the Cowboy Poetry Gathering in Elko.

Arts and Crafts: Outdoor Art Festival (Boulder), Cowboy Poetry Gathering (Elko), Western Art Round-Up (Winnemucca).

Music: Artemus W. Ham Concert Hall (Las Vegas), International Jazz Festival (Reno), Nevada Opera (Reno).

Entertainment: Battle Mountain Annual Crab Feed and Dance (Battle Mountain), Boulder Damboree (Boulder), Lincoln County Homecoming (Caliente), Meadow Valley Western Days (Caliente), Kit Carson Rendezvous/Wagon Train Days (Carson City), Spring Fun Fair (Carson City), Nevada Day Celebration (Carson City), Cowboy Poetry Gathering (Elko), National Basque Festival (Elko), Mardi Gras (Elko), County Fair and Livestock Show (Elko), Pony Express Days (Ely), White Pine County Fair (Ely), Carson Valley Days (Gardnerville), Industrial Days (Henderson), Lake Mead Parade of Lights (Lake Mead), All Indian Powwow (Las Vegas), Helldorado Festival (Las Vegas), Jaycee State Fair (Las Vegas), Jerry Lewis Telethon (Las Vegas), Laughlin River Days (Laughlin), Frontier Days (Lovelock), Heritage Days (Pioche), Sparks Festival Days (Sparks), Jim Butler Days (Tonopah), Red Mountain Powwow (Winnemucca).

Tours: Lincoln County Art Room (Caliente), Hidden Cave Tours (Fallon), Ichthyosaur Fossil Shelter (Gabbs), Piper's Opera House (Virginia City).

Theater: Judy Bayley Theatre (Las Vegas), Reed Whipple Cultural Center (Las Vegas), Charleston Heights Arts Center (Las Vegas), Church Fine Arts Theatre (Reno).

Rodeos are popular attractions throughout Nevada.

Considered one of the most beautiful places in the world, Lake Tahoe on the border of California and Nevada, has been a popular vacation resort for more than a century.

The Land and the Climate

Nevada is bounded on the west by California, on the north by Oregon and Idaho, on the east by Utah and Arizona, and on the south by California. The state has three main land areas: the Columbia Plateau, the Sierra Nevada, and the Basin and Range Region.

The Columbia Plateau lies along Nevada's northern border. It is a small strip of land that reaches from the middle of the state to the Utah boundary line. Deep lava bedrock lies below the surface of the region, and streams and rivers have cut deep canyons here. Some sheep ranches are found in the area, which is unsuitable for farming.

The Sierra Nevada is part of a rugged mountain range that cuts across the southwestern corner of the state. This small area includes Lake Tahoe and other scenic mountain lakes that are popular tourist resorts.

Most of Nevada is within the arid Basin and Range Region. This is an upland area containing many mountain ranges that extend from north to south, including the Sierra Nevada, Toiyabe, Toquima, Snake, and Toana Ranges. Between the ranges are buttes—steep, solitary hills—and mesas, which are tablelike mountains. There are also many valleys and alkalai flats in the region. Elevations range from 500 feet above sea level to more than 13,000 feet. Near the California border is 13,140-foot Boundary Peak, the highest point in Nevada. Farming, ranching, and mining are the chief economic activities. Irrigation makes it possible to raise wheat, hay, barley, grapes and other fruit, and vegetables. Livestock includes beef and dairy cattle, hogs, poultry, and sheep. The region is rich in mineral resources, including mercury, tungsten, gold, iron, silver, magnesium, beryllium, copper, zinc, and lead.

Lake Mead was created by the Hoover Dam and is the largest water project in the state.

Most of Nevada's rivers are dry for part of the year and flow only from December to June. The most important rivers in the state are the Colorado, Virgin, Muddy, Owyhee, Bruneau, Salmon, Humboldt, Carson, Walker, and Truckee. Many beautiful lakes are found in the mountainous west-central part of the state.

The Valley of Fire State Park is named for the great formations of red sandstone, such as Elephant Rock, that are found there.

Wheeler Peak in the Great Basin National Park stands over 13,000 feet.

Nevada receives less rain than any other state—the maximum is seven inches—largely because of the Sierra Nevada, whose lofty peaks cause clouds moving inland from the Pacific to drop much of their moisture in the form of snow. Snowfall in the Sierra often reaches more than 200 inches per year. Temperatures in Nevada vary greatly from north to south, averaging 70 degrees Fahrenheit in July in the mountains and over 85 degrees F. in the south. In winter, the mountains average 24 degrees F. and southern Nevada, 43 degrees F.

The History

John Charles Frémont (1813–90) explored the Nevada territory in several expeditions during the 1840s.

What is now Nevada was home to some of North America's earliest inhabitants. Excavation of bones, ashes, and other remains near Las Vegas indicates that people lived in the area at least 10,000 years ago. There, and in southern Nevada, Paleo-Indians left picture writing (petroglyphs) on the rock walls of their caves. Ancestors of today's Pueblo Indians, called Basketmakers, lived at Lovelock cave and in the Las Vegas area. When the Spanish arrived in the 1700s, they found the Mohave, Paiute, Shoshone, and Washoe tribes.

The first European to visit the Nevada region was probably the Spanish missionary Francisco Garcés, who passed through the territory around 1775 while traveling from New Mexico to California. Nevada was claimed by Spain as an extension of its holdings in New Spain (Mexico). Some 50 years after Garcés arrived, fur trappers and traders began to explore the region. Most of them were from the British Hudson's Bay Company. In 1826 the American trader Jedediah S. Smith crossed the Las Vegas Valley region into California with a group of trappers.

In 1830 William Wolfskill blazed the route called the Old Spanish Trail from Santa Fe to Los Angeles, passing through the Nevada region, which had been largely isolated by the high mountains on either side of it. Three years later, Joseph Walker marked out a trail through the Humboldt River Valley that would soon be traveled by thousands of prospectors seeking gold in California. In the mid-1840s, the John C. Frémont expeditions, guided by Kit Carson, resulted in maps and accurate information about Nevada. By now the region had become part of Mexico, which threw off Spanish rule in 1821.

In 1846 the United States and Mexico went to war for title to a vast region that included Nevada, California, Utah, and parts of four other states. When the war ended in an American victory in 1848, settlers began coming into the region, first from Utah, where Brigham Young had established the Church of Jesus Christ of Latter-day Saints (the Mormons) on the Great Salt Lake. In 1849 they set up a trading post called Mormon Station near what is now Genoa. Young had organized Utah and most of Nevada into the State of Deseret, and he asked the federal government to admit it to the Union. Instead, the government created the Utah Territory, with Young as governor, in 1850.

The outpost at Mormon Station supplied prospectors heading for California, and additional Mormon families soon came into the Carson Valley to farm and raise livestock. Non-Mormon settlers in Nevada began to feel that they were in the minority, and they tried to persuade Congress to create a separate territory for them, or to make them part of the California Territory, at first without success. Then, in 1859, a rich vein of silver ore was discovered near what is now Virginia City. Prospector Henry Comstock took credit for the find, although it turned out that others had made the discovery.

Virginia City, once the richest mining town in the west, attracts tourists with its old-fashioned saloons, wooden sidewalks, and Victorian mansions built with the wealth of the Comstock Lode.

Nevertheless, it went down in history as the Comstock Lode, which proved to be rich in gold as well as silver. Treasure hunters and adventurers poured into Carson County, where they set up lawless tent towns. Almost overnight, Virginia City became a thriving mining center.

By 1860 the mining camps, populated by prospectors living in tents, caves, and stone huts, held more than 6,000 people. In March of the following year, President James Buchanan signed an act establishing the Nevada Territory. When President Abraham Lincoln took office two days later, he appointed James W. Nye, a New York City politician, governor of the territory. But the Civil War broke out before Nevada's territorial government could be set up in Carson City.

Mining camps were a common sight in the Nevada Territory, in the mid-1800s.

Most Nevadans favored the Union cause, and the territory's silver and gold deposits made it attractive to the North, faced with the cost of waging the war. But Nevada was far short of the 127,381 citizens required by law to become a state. Nevertheless, a state constitution was drawn up with Congressional approval, and Nevada was admitted to the Union as the 36th state in 1864. Nine years later, the richest strike of gold and silver in the history of mining was made near Virginia City—"the Big Bonanza."

For the next 30 years, Nevada's economy went up and down with the value of silver. Mines were soon tapped-out, or produced only low-grade ore, and as the government's demand for silver fell, people were forced to leave the state or to take up ranching. Nevada's population dropped from about 62,000 in 1880 to some 47,000 in 1890. Mines closed, and several thriving communities turned into ghost towns.

During the early 1900s, new deposits of silver, copper, and gold were found in Nevada, and a second wave of prospectors arrived. This time, railroad spur lines extended into mining areas, and cattlemen used them to transport their livestock more economically. The land was being irrigated, with help from the federal government, which still owns 97 percent of the state. When the United States entered World War I in 1917, the richest of Nevada's gold and silver deposits were running out. But the state's copper, tungsten, and other minerals were bringing top prices for wartime weapons construction.

Work began on the Boulder Dam (now Hoover Dam) in 1930. This huge project on the Colorado River was completed in 1936, and the 726-foot-high dam provided both electric power and irrigation water for the region.

As early as 1869, the state legislature had permitted games of chance in Nevada, but laws against gambling had been passed by 1910. However, it was difficult to enforce the laws, and gamblers were seldom caught or convicted. The people of Nevada came to believe that it was cheaper to legalize gambling than to try to stop it, and they did this in 1931. Large casinos were built, and people traveled to Nevada from other states where gambling was illegal. State laws that made it easy to obtain a divorce also brought thousands of people to Nevada each year until permissive divorce laws were passed nationwide.

Nevada mines were booming again during World War II. Manufacturers of military supplies needed the state's copper, lead, magnesite, manganese, tungsten, and zinc. Some of the ghost towns came to life again as the mines reopened. When the war ended in 1945, the demand for these minerals went down, but some of the mining communities moved into chemical manufacturing. In the 1950s, the U.S. Atomic Energy Commission conducted studies in the state, and Nellis Air Force Base, used for weapons testing, was established in North Las Vegas. Atomic energy then became an important Nevada industry.

Today more and more industries are coming into Nevada, including electronics and chemical companies. Gambling and tourism are still big businesses, centered in Las Vegas and Reno. Nevada's reputation for gambling and glamorous nightlife is balanced by its rich history, magnificent desert scenery, and soundly based economy.

Reno, a popular gambling center, is close to Lake Tahoe and many of the state's excellent recreational facilities.

The Basque Festival, celebrating that distinct ethnic group from the Pyrenees, is held in Elko every July and features traditional dancing.

Education

Nevadans made plans for a tax-supported school system as early as 1861, when the region became a territory. The first school districts were set up in 1865. The University of Nevada at Reno was established in 1874, and its Las Vegas branch was founded in 1957.

The People

More than 82 percent of the people in Nevada live in metropolitan areas such as Las Vegas and Reno. About 91 percent of them were born in the United States. More than 20 percent of Nevadans are Roman Catholics, and another 20 percent belong to the Church of Jesus Christ of Latter-day Saints (the Mormons). Other sizable religious groups include the Baptists, Episcopalians, Jews, Lutherans, Methodists, and Presbyterians.

Native Nevadans are descended mainly from hardy American pioneers who had to contend with deserts, mountains, isolation, and a prevailing scarcity of water. Nevada's hectic mining boom-town days were chronicled by Missouri-born Mark Twain (Samuel Clemens), who went to Carson City with his brother Orion Clement, secretary of the Territory of Nevada, in 1861. Twain's humorous memoir *Roughing It*, published in 1872, became a classic and increased national awareness of Nevada.

During the early 1900s, Nevada was among the first states to adopt such progressive measures as woman suffrage (voting rights) and the referendum, by which proposed laws are submitted to a direct popular vote. In 1979 Nevada enacted legislation designed to increase its control over land owned by the federal government, in what was called "the Sagebrush Revolt."

Senator Paul Laxalt, once the Republican Governor of Nevada, is of Basque descent.

Famous People

Many famous people were born in the state of Nevada. Here are a few:

Eva B. Adams 1908-91, Wonder. Director of U.S. Mint

Henry Fountain Ashurst 1874-1962, Winnemucca. Senate leader

Jack Kramer b. 1921, Las Vegas. Champion tennis player

Paul Laxalt b. 1922, Reno. Senate leader

Robert C. Lynch 1880-1931, Carson City. Surgeon

Anne H. Martin 1875-1951, Empire City. Suffragist, author, and social critic

Pat McCarran 1876-1954, near Reno. Senate leader

Max McGee b. 1932, Saxton City. Football player

Maurice E. McLoughlin 1890-1957, Carson City. Champion tennis player

Charles Michelson 1868-1948, Virginia City. Journalist and political publicist

Jim Nash b. 1945, Hawthorne. Baseball pitcher

Pat Nixon 1912-93, Ely. Former first lady.

Mark L. Requa 1865-1937, Virginia City. Mining engineer and political leader

Sarah Winnemucca 1844-91, near Humboldt Lake. Indian scout and interpreter

Wovoka 1856-1932, near Walker Lake. Indian mystic and originator of Ghost Dance religion

Colleges and Universities

Here are the locations, dates of founding, and enrollments at some of the universities in the state of Nevada.

Morrison College, Reno, 1902, 280

Sierra Nevada College, Incline Village, 1969, 530

University of Nevada, Las Vegas, Las Vegas, 1957, 19,504

University of Nevada, Reno, Reno, 1874, 11,909

Where To Get More Information

Nevada Commission on Tourism
Capitol Complex
Carson City NV 89710
Or call 1-800-NEVADA8

Utah

The state seal of Utah, adopted in 1896, is circular. In the center is a shield with a beehive, representing industry. To the left and right of the beehive are sego lilies, standing for peace. Below the beehive is the date 1847, the year the Mormons came to the Salt Lake Valley. The top of the shield is pierced by six arrows, under which is the word *Industry* on a banner. Over the shield is an American eagle with outstretched wings, and to each side of the shield is an American flag. Around the seal is printed "The Great Seal of the State of Utah" and "1896," the year Utah became a state.

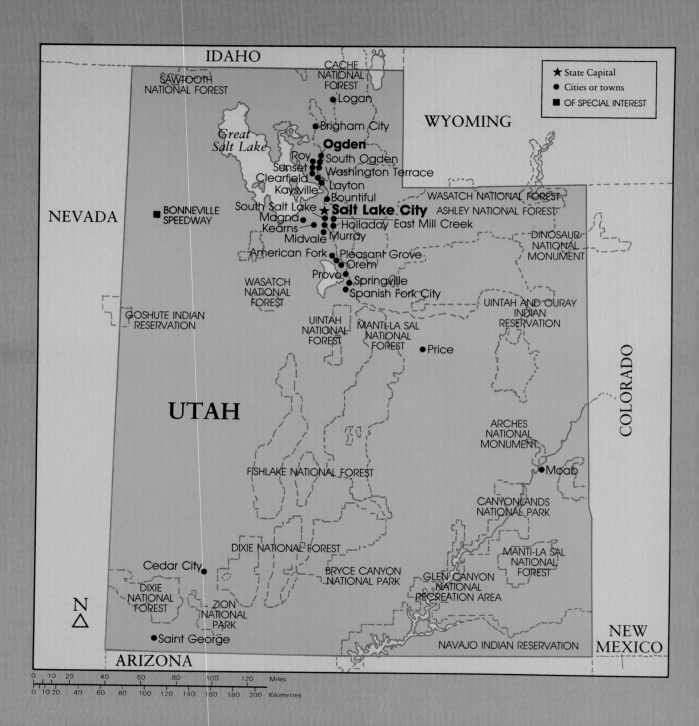

UTAH
At a Glance

Capital: Salt Lake City

State Flag

State Bird: Seagull

Size: 84,899 square miles (11th largest)
Population: 1,813,116 (34th largest)

State Flower: Sego Lily

Major Industries: Guided missiles, electronic components, metals
Major Crops: Wheat, hay, apples, barley, corn, potatoes

State Flag

The state flag of Utah was adopted in 1913. On a blue field is the shield, eagle, and American flags from the state seal. Below the shield are the dates 1847 and 1896. A narrow gold circle surrounds the seal.

State Motto

Industry

The motto was adopted in 1896.

Colorful hot air balloons cross the Utah sky.

State Capital

Salt Lake City has been the capital since 1856, forty years before Utah became a state.

State Name and Nicknames

The White Mountain Apache Indians called the Navajo *Yuttahih,* which meant "one that is higher up." But early explorers thought that the word referred to the Ute, who lived higher in the mountains, so the land of the Utes became Utah.

The most common nickname for Utah is the *Beehive State,* the symbol of industry on the state seal and flag. Because it was settled by the Mormons, it is also called the *Mormon State* and the *Land of the Saints* (the Mormon church is officially called The Church of Jesus Christ of the Latter-Day Saints). Because of the Great Salt Lake, it is also referred to as the *Salt Lake State.*

State Flower

The sego lily, *Calochortus nuttalli,* was named the state flower of Utah in 1911.

Sunset over the Great Salt Lake.

State Tree

The blue spruce, *Picea pungens,* was selected as state tree in 1933.

State Bird

In 1955, the legislature adopted the California gull, *Larus californicus,* as state bird.

State Animal

The elk, *Cervus canadensis,* has been the state animal since 1971.

State Emblem

The beehive was named state emblem in 1959.

State Fish

The rainbow trout, *Salmo irideus,* was selected as the state fish in 1971.

State Gem

The topaz has been the state gem since 1969.

State Insect

The honeybee, *Apis mellifera,* was selected as state insect in 1983.

Rocket boosters under construction at the Morton Thiokol plant.

State Song

In 1937, "Utah We Love Thee," written by Evan Stephens, was adopted as the state song.

Population

The population of Utah in 1992 was 1,813,116, making it the 34th most populous state. There are 20.29 people per square mile.

Industries

The principal industries of Utah are services, trade, manufacturing, government, and construction.

The chief manufactured products are guided missiles and parts, electronic components, food products, fabricated metals, steel, and electrical equipment.

The Kennecott copper mine is one of many in Utah.

Agriculture

The chief crops of the state are wheat, hay, apples, barley, alfalfa seed, corn, potatoes, cherries, and onions. Utah is also a livestock state. There are estimated to be some 855,000 cattle, 34,000 hogs and pigs, 600,000 sheep, and 3.8 million chickens and turkeys on its farms. Aspen, spruce, and pine trees are harvested. Copper, gold, and magnesium are important mineral resources.

Government

The governor of Utah is elected to a four-year term, as are the attorney general, lieutenant governor, state auditor, and state treasurer. The state legislature, which meets annually, consists of a 29-member senate and a 75-member house of representatives. Senators serve four-year terms and representatives serve two-year terms. They are elected from districts drawn up according to population. The

most recent state constitution was adopted in 1895. In addition to its two U.S. senators, Utah has three representatives in the House of Representatives. The state has five votes in the electoral college.

Sports

Sports are popular in Utah. On the collegiate level, the NCAA basketball championship was won by the University of Utah in 1944. The National Invitation Tournament was won by the University of Utah (1947) and Brigham Young University (1951, 1966). On the professional level, the Utah Jazz of the National Basketball Association play in the Salt Palace in Salt Lake City.

Major Cities

Ogden (population 63,943). Settled in 1844, Ogden was laid out by Brigham Young in a geometrical style. Named after fur trader Peter Ogden, its superb location equidistant from all major west coast cities made Ogden a railroad center and transcontinental junction. Today it remains important due to its location and is utilized as a military supply center. The railroads continue to employ many people. It also is a commercial and industrial center.

Things to see in Ogden: Daughters of Utah Pioneers Visitors Center and Relic Hall, Union Station, Browning-Kimball Car Museum, Browning Firearms Museum, Pine View Reservoir, and Fort Buenaventura State Park.

Provo (population 86,835). Settled in 1849, this city, surrounded by high mountains, is an education and commercial center. It was named after the French-Canadian explorer Etienne Provost, who explored the area in 1825.

Things to see in Provo: Secured Art Gallery, Harris Fine Arts Center, Eyring Science Center, Monte L. Bean Life Science Museum, Museum of Peoples and Cultures, McCurdy Historical Doll Museum, Pioneer Museum, Camp Floyd State Park, and Bridal Veil Falls Tramway.

Karl "the Mailman" Malone, of the Utah Jazz. The team relocated from New Orleans in 1979 and has yet to change its nickname.

The Mormon Tabernacle in Salt Lake City is famous for its fine acoustics.

The Lion House was built in 1856 as a home for part of Brigham Young's large family.

Salt Lake City (population 159,928). Founded in 1847, the capital city, once the site of a desert wilderness, is a monument to the invincibility of the human spirit. The most populous city in Utah, it is often referred to as the "Mormon Capital." The Gold Rush of 1849 brought many people to this region as gold prospectors and speculators rushed to the West Coast through Salt Lake City. Lacking money, these gold rushers traded with the Mormons for necessary supplies. Started as a farming community, Salt Lake City has become an economically successful city with industry, commerce, mining, and finance. The land that is now called Salt Lake City was hard and dry when the Mormons first occupied this region. Mountain streams were diverted to soften the land and it eventually became suitable for farming. The Salt Lake Valley remains a profitable agricultural region, producing meat and dairy products. It was laid out in a grid pattern and today is an industrious, businesslike city.

Things to see in Salt Lake City: Temple Square, Tabernacle (1867), Temple (1893, closed to non-Mormons), Assembly Hall (1882), Seagull Monument (1913), Museum of Church History and Art, Family History Library, Salt Palace, Arrow Press Square, Lion House (1856), Beehive House (1854), State Capitol (1914), Council Hall, Governor's Mansion, Pioneer Memorial Museum, Carriage House, Hansen Planetarium (1905), ZCMI (Zion's Co-operative Mercantile Institution), Salt Lake Art Center, Utah Museum of Fine Arts, Utah Museum of Natural History, State Arboretum, Trolley Square, Liberty Park, Raging Waters, "This Is the Place" Monument, Old Deseret Pioneer Village, Hogle Zoological Garden, 49th Street Galleria, Fort Douglas Military Museum, and Wheeler Historic Farm.

Places to Visit

The National Park Service maintains 21 areas in the state of Utah: Arches National Park, Bryce Canyon National Park, Canyonlands National Park, Capitol Reef National Park, Zion National Park, Cedar Breaks National Monument, Dinosaur National Monument, Natural Bridges National Monument, Rainbow Bridge National Monument, Timpanogos

Capitol Reef National Park consists of eroded rocks of unusual shapes and colors.

Cave National Monument, Hovenweep National Monument, Golden Spike National Historic Site, High Uintahs Wilderness Area, most of Glen Canyon National Recreation Area, most of Flaming Gorge Dam and National Recreation Area, Ashley National Forest, Dixie National Forest, Fishlake National Forest, Manti-LaSal National Forest, Uintah National Forest, and Wasatch-Cache National Forest. In addition, there are 29 state recreation areas.

Boulder: Anasazi Indian Village State Park. Visitors may tour the site where 87 rooms dating from A.D. 1050 have been excavated.

Brigham City: Brigham City Mormon Tabernacle. Built in 1881, this house of worship is still in use.

Cedar City: Iron Mission State Park. An extensive collection of pioneer horse-drawn vehicles and wagons is on display here, the site of the first iron foundry west of the Mississippi.

Farmington: Lagoon Amusement Park. This park features a replica of a 19th-century frontier settlement, stagecoach rides, and wild West entertainment.

Fillmore: Territorial Statehouse State Park. Utah's first territorial capitol is now a museum.

Green River: Goblin Valley State Park. This mile-wide basin is filled with oddly-eroded sandstone formations.

Heber City: Heber Creeper. Visitors may take a train ride through Heber Valley and Provo Canyon.

Kanab: Movie sets. Several movie locations can be seen in the area, including a false-front Western town.

Lehi: John Hutching's Museum of Natural History. The museum contains pioneer and Indian artifacts, fossils, a large mineral collection, and shell and bird specimens.

Logan: Ronald V. Jensen Historical Farm and Man and His Bread Museum. This re-creation of a typical pioneer farm includes exhibits on agricultural development

Goblin Valley is preserved as a Utah state park.

from the mid-1800s to the present.

Moab: Hollywood Stuntmen's Hall of Fame. Exhibits include stuntmen's costumes, weapons, photographs, and videos.

Park City: Egyptian Theatre.

Built in 1926, it was originally a silent-film theater and vaudeville house.

Price: College of Eastern Utah Prehistoric Museum. Displays of dinosaur remains and geological specimens are featured.

St. George: Brigham Young Winter Home. Built in 1873, this adobe home was used by Young during his last nine winters.

Springville: Springville Museum of Art. Exhibits feature works by Utah artists.

Vacationers hit the slopes of one of Utah's many fine ski resorts.

A snow sculpture rises majestically from the icy Utah winterscape.

Vernal: Utah Field House of Natural History. The gardens are designed to appear as they did during the age of the dinosaurs and contain 14 life-size dinosaur figures.

Events

There are many events and organizations that schedule activities of various kinds in the state of Utah. Here are some of them.

Sports: Golden Circle Marathon (Blanding), Utah Summer Games (Cedar City), Rodeos and horse races (Cedar City), Cutter, snowmobile, and dog sled races (Heber City), Rodeo (Kanab), Rod Run and Chili Cook-Off (Lake Powell), Steam Threshing Bee (Logan), Canyonlands Festival and Rodeo (Moab), Winter Sun Run-10K Race (Moab), Canyonlands PRCA Rodeo/Butch Cassidy Days (Moab), Pioneer Days Rodeo (Ogden), Horse racing (Panguitch), Snow Sculpture Contest (Park City), Ride and Tie (Park City), Showdown Classic/Jeremy Ranch (Park City), Drag Races/Dixie Raceway (St. George), Dinosaur Roundup Rodeo (Vernal), Water Skiing Competition (Vernal), Bonneville National Speed Trials (Wendover), Western Stampede (West Jordan).

Arts and Crafts: Utah Pageant of the Arts (American Fork), Bluff Indian Day (Bluff), Peach Day Celebration (Brigham City), Rock, Gem and Mineral Show (Moab), Art Festival (Park City), Utah Arts Festival (Salt Lake City), National Quilt Show (Springville).

Music: American Folk Ballet Summer Festival (Cedar City), Utah Symphony Pops Concert (Ogden), Temple Square Christmas (Salt Lake City), Utah Opera Company (Salt Lake City), Ballet West (Salt Lake City), Ririe-Woodbury Dance Company (Salt Lake City), Repertory Dance Theatre (Salt Lake City), Utah Symphony (Salt

Two children enjoy themselves at the Park City Art Festival.

Lake City), Utah Symphony (Snowbird).

Entertainment: New Year's Eve Torchlight Parade and Fireworks (Brian Head), Driving of Golden Spike (Brigham City), Railroaders Festival (Brigham City), Highland Heritage Festival (Cedar City), Midsummer Renaissance Faire (Cedar City), Tintic-Silver Festival (Eureka), Melon Days (Green River), Friendship Cruise (Green River), Wasatch County Fair (Heber City), Swiss Days (Heber City), Desert Vagabond Days (Kanab), Festival of the American West (Logan), Cache County Fair (Logan), Swiss Christmas (Midway), Jeep Safari (Moab), Friendship Cruise (Moab), Monticello Pioneer Days (Monticello), San Juan County 4-H Fair (Monticello), National Western Film Festival (Ogden), Winter Fest (Ogden), Miner's Day Celebration (Park City), United States Film Festival (Park City), Autumn Aloft Hot Air Balloon Festival (Park City), Salmon supper (Payson), Golden Onion Days (Payson), Freedom

Festival (Provo), Washington County Fair (St. George), Dixie Roundup (St. George), Pioneer Christmas Days (Salt Lake City), Utah State Fair (Salt Lake City), Day's of '47 Celebration (Salt Lake City), World Folkfest (Springville), Outlaw Trail Festival (Vernal), Southern Utah Folklife Festival (Zion National Park).

Tours: Jeep Jamboree (Blanding), Guided Pack Trips and Mountain Trail Rides

(Kamas), Wagons West (St. George).

Theater: Utah Shakespearian Festival (Cedar City), Shakespeare Festival (Park City), Egyptian Theatre (Park City), Pageant of the Arts (Provo), Pioneer Players (St. George), Mormon Miracle Pageant (Salina), Pioneer Memorial Theatre (Salt Lake City), The "Promised Valley" (Salt Lake City), Utah Arts Festival (Salt Lake City).

Utah's scenic freshwater lakes provide fishing and other outdoor activities.

The Land and the Climate

Utah is bounded on the west by Nevada, on the north by Idaho and Wyoming, on the east by Wyoming and Colorado, and on the south by Arizona. There are three major land regions in the state: the Rocky Mountains, the Basin and Range Region, and the Colorado Plateau.

The Uinta Range of the Rocky Mountains is in northeastern Utah, near the Colorado and Wyoming borders. The rest of Utah's Rocky Mountains Region is formed by the north-south Wasatch Range. Near the center of the Uinta Range is Kings Peak, which is 13,498 feet above sea level—the highest point in Utah. Many lakes and canyons formed by ancient glaciers occur in the Rockies, and the steep Wasatch Range has several deep canyons cut by rivers. The region supports sheep and cattle ranches, and dairy farms. Crops grown here include barley, alfalfa, and vegetables.

Bryce Canyon National Park is filled with delicate spires of sandstone.

Lake Powell in the Glen Canyon National Recreational Area was created by a dam on the Colorado River.

The Basin and Range Region of western Utah is part of a large dry area that Utah shares with several other states. Small mountain ranges alternate with broad basins from which streams have no outlets. The Great Salt Lake and the desert of the same name are in the northern part of this region. Lead, zinc, copper, silver, iron, and gold are mined here. Farms and ranches produce beef cattle, potatoes, sugar beets, wheat, and barley.

The Colorado Plateau covers parts of Utah, Arizona, Colorado, and New Mexico; in Utah, it forms most of the state's eastern side. On the plateau, broad uplands are cut by deep canyons, the most famous of which are Bryce, Cedar Breaks, and Zion Canyons. This is a region of oil and natural gas wells, cattle ranches, alfalfa farms, and coal and uranium mines.

The rivers of Utah are especially important for irrigation, without which much of the state would be a desert. The most important rivers are the Colorado and the Green, followed by the Snake, Bear, Provo, Weber, and Sevier. Great Salt Lake is the largest natural lake west of the Mississippi River, and it is four to five times saltier than the oceans. This is caused by the lack of drainage by outflowing streams. When the water evaporates, it leaves a residue of salt behind.

Differences in temperature of up to 20 degrees occur between northern and southern Utah. July averages in Salt Lake City range from 60 degrees Fahrenheit to 92 degrees F. January temperatures range between 17 and 36 degrees F. Up to 400 inches of snow may fall in the mountainous ski areas, while southern Utah receives only a few inches per year.

The Doll House is one of the extraordinary formations in the Canyonlands National Park, south of Moab.

The History

Jim Bridger (1804–81), the fur trader and scout, is thought to be the first white man to visit the Great Salt Lake.

Utah's first inhabitants were nomadic cave dwellers who roamed the Southwest thousands of years ago. By the time of Christ, a people now known as the Basketmakers, for their weaving skill with plant fibers, were living in communities and growing squash and corn. After about A.D. 400 they were making pottery and from about A.D. 700 they began to build elaborate cliff dwellings. The Navajo later called these early people the Anasazi, or Ancient Ones. Their descendants were the Pueblo Indians who today live farther south.

In 1776 Spanish explorers found four major tribes—the Gosiute, Paiute, Shoshone (or the Snake), and Ute, who gave the state their name. Years later, nomadic Navajo Indians came into the region; they still live in many parts of the state.

It is possible that the Spanish explorers who discovered the Grand Canyon of the Colorado River in 1540 traveled from the Arizona region into Utah, but historians are not sure. It is known that in 1776, while America was waging the Revolutionary War against Great Britain, two Spanish Franciscan friars entered the territory. These missionaries, Silvestre Velez de Escalante and Francisco Atanasio Domínguez, discovered Utah Lake, southeast of the Great Salt Lake.

Although Spain claimed the Utah region as part of New Spain (Mexico), no colonies were established. A few American fur traders explored the area in 1811 and 1812, but it was Jim Bridger, the frontier scout, who aroused interest in the territory in 1825. He was probably the first American to see the Great Salt Lake. Because of the water's salty taste, he thought he had found an ocean.

Bridger's reports brought hundreds of fur trappers and traders into Utah, and by 1830 the region was well traveled. But the travelers were mainly transients, on their way from Santa Fe to Los Angeles.

The founder of the Mormon Church, Joseph Smith (1805–44), preached to his followers from the back of a wagon during their search for a permanent settlement.

In 1847 members of the Church of Jesus Christ of Latter-day Saints (the Mormons) arrived in Utah. The church had been founded in Fayette, New York, in 1830 by Joseph Smith. Its members had been persecuted almost everywhere they went, due largely to their practice of polygamy, by which a man could have more than one wife. Looking for religious freedom, they had traveled to Ohio and Missouri. Unwelcome there, they went to Illinois, where they were forcibly expelled from Nauvoo in 1846. When Smith was killed in Illinois, Brigham Young became the leader of 12,000 Mormons and headed west with his followers.

In 1847 the Mormons reached Utah, and an advance party encamped in the forbidding land around the Great Salt Lake and began to plow the rocklike soil and build a dam for irrigation water. When Young arrived with the rest of the expedition and saw the land they were to settle, he said, "If there is a place on this earth that nobody else wants, that's the place I am hunting for." Perhaps never before in human history has such hard work and intelligence been applied to the problem of converting a barren wilderness into lush, productive land. What the Mormons did not have, they did without or made themselves. Every member extended himself for the good of the community.

The Mormons founded a state named Deseret, which included much of present-day Nevada, and spread out from their original settlement of Salt Lake City. They established several other communities in which they irrigated, farmed, and raised livestock. Because they needed cotton, they sent families south to St. George and established Utah's "Dixie." In 1848 the northern valleys were invaded by huge swarms of grasshoppers, which started to destroy the crops. But seagulls from the Great Salt Lake ended the plague of insects—and established their claim as the official state bird.

The Mormons' Perpetual Emigrating Fund was set up in 1849. The money in the fund was used to bring other Mormons into the area, especially those who could not afford to make the trip on their own.

Brigham Young (1801–77) joined the Mormon Church in 1832. He became president of the Council of the Twelve Apostles in 1844 and led the Latter-day Saints westward to establish the state of Deseret on the banks of the Great Salt Lake.

About 50,000 new settlers were brought west by the fund, including some from Denmark, England, Norway, Scotland, Sweden, and Wales, where Mormon missionaries had made converts.

The settlements prospered, and at first they enjoyed peaceful relationships with the Indians. But controversies over land ownership led to conflicts in the 1850s and 1860s. In 1853 a Ute chief named Walker led attacks against several of the settlements in what was known as the Walker War. The following year, Young persuaded Walker to end the fighting. A period of peace lasted until 1865, when another Ute chief, Black Hawk, led an uprising against the Mormons. When other tribes joined him, the Black Hawk War began. About 50 settlers were killed, and the Mormons lost more than a million dollars worth of property. The war ended in 1867, with discussions between the Mormons and the Indians at Mount Pleasant, in Sanpete County. The disagreements were settled on Brigham Young's advice that it would be less costly to feed the Indians than to fight them, and most of the Ute settled on a reservation in the Uinta Basin.

When the Mormons arrived in 1847, the Utah region belonged to Mexico, which was at war with the United States for most of the Southwest. When the United States won the war in 1848, Utah became American territory. In 1849 the Mormons made Brigham Young governor of the State of Deseret and asked to be admitted to the Union. Instead, the region was designated the Utah Territory, with Young as governor. The Mormons asked for statehood several times, but were refused because of their practice of polygamy, although only a small number of men had more than one wife. In the meantime, the federal government tried to weaken Mormon control of the territory.

In 1857 President James Buchanan appointed Alfred Cummings of Georgia, a non-Mormon, the territorial governor, deposing Young. Soldiers marched toward Utah to enforce the appointment. A group of Utah Mormons and Indians were waiting for the troops, but so nervous were they that they attacked a party of travelers who were simply passing through. Most of the 140 travelers were killed in what became known as the Mountain Meadows Massacre.

It wasn't until 1858 that the U.S. troops arrived, after wintering outside the state. Jim Bridger was their guide. The soldiers stayed for three years, and although no battles were fought, it was a tense period that became known as the Utah, or Mormon, War. The troops left when the Civil War broke out in 1861.

The federal government still hoped to wrest control of Utah from the Mormons. The discovery of gold in 1863 seemed to promise a rush of non-Mormon settlers, but they had little impact on the strongly entrenched community. The Pony Express crossed Utah on route from St. Joseph, Missouri, to Sacramento, California, in 1860 and 1861. Then the first transcontinental telegraph service linked Utah with the East and West Coasts. In 1869 the Central Pacific

The Pony Express, the first transcontinental mail service, which ran from April 1860 to October 1861, crossed the Utah Territory.

The "Golden Spike" linking the Central Pacific Railroad from Sacramento, California and the Union Pacific Railroad from Omaha, Nebraska, was driven at Promontory Point in Utah in 1869.

railroad, laying track from Sacramento, met the track laid by the Union Pacific Railroad from Omaha, Nebraska, at Promontory, Utah. The nation's first transcontinental railroad became a reality.

During the 1880s, the federal government began to enforce a law against polygamy that had been passed in 1862. Many Mormons were sent to prison. In 1887 Congress passed a law permitting the government to seize Mormon church property to be used for public education. In 1890 the Mormons finally capitulated and prohibited the practice of polygamy.

In 1895 Utah tried again to become a state, submitting a new constitution that outlawed polygamy and prohibited control of the state by any religious group. In 1896 Utah was admitted as the 45th state of the Union.

During the next 35 years, railroad building boomed, mining operations expanded, and farmland increased with improved irrigation technology. Beef cattle soon became important to Utah's economy. During World War I, state mines supplied the government with large quantities of metals, especially copper. But these gains were almost canceled out by the Great Depression of the 1930s. Farm prices dropped, and Utah had one of the nation's highest unemployment rates.

The economic demands of World War II put the state back on its feet. Between 1939 and 1945, the value of manufacturing nearly tripled, and Utah became one of the nation's largest suppliers of copper, gold, lead, silver, and zinc. Steel-product manufacturing came into the picture after the war. Oil production and refining came to the fore, and uranium mining boomed.

Today the state's industries are still growing, including electronics, primary metals, and transportation equipment. Tourism is a multimillion-dollar business because of Utah's magnificent national parks, campgrounds, and sporting facilities. The state is one of monumental beauty, with mountains, lakes, canyons, and forests. It is a land seemingly created for those who love the Western outdoors and can appreciate the awesome accomplishments of the pioneers who developed it.

Education

The first school in Utah was set up in a tent in the Salt Lake Valley in 1847, the year of the Mormons' first settlement. In less than 10 years, Utah had more than 200 schools. The first free public high schools were mandated in 1895. Today Utah has the highest percentage of high-school graduates in the country, and a larger percentage of its population attends college than in any other state. When the first shipment of books arrived in the 1850s, the library that would become the Utah State Library was founded. In 1898 the first free public library opened in Salt Lake City. By the time Utah became a state in 1896, it had five institutions of higher education.

The great Temple, sacred to the Mormons, stands in Temple Square in Salt Lake City. A statue of the angel Moroni is perched on the highest of the three spires.

Square dancing is a popular pastime in Utah.

The People

Approximately 77 percent of Utahans live in metropolitan areas such as Salt Lake City and Provo. More than 96 percent of them were born in the United States. The largest groups from other countries came from Canada, England, Germany, and the Netherlands. More than 60 percent of the state's people belong to the Church of Jesus Christ of Latter-day Saints (the Mormons). Utah also has many Baptists, Episcopalians, Methodists, Presbyterians, and Roman Catholics.

Famous People

Many famous people were born in the state of Utah. Here are a few:

Maude Adams 1872-1953, Salt Lake City. Stage actress

Florence E. Allen 1884-1966, Salt Lake City. First woman appointed to a U.S. court of appeals

Solon Hannibal Borglum 1868-1922, Ogden. Sculptor

Frank Borzage 1893-1962, Salt Lake City. Film director

John Moses Browning 1855-1926, Ogden. Firearms designer

Virgil Carter b. 1945, Anabella. Football quarterback

Tom Chambers b. 1959, Ogden. Basketball player

Joshua R. Clark, Jr. 1871-1961, Grantsville. Lawyer, diplomat and churchman

Cyrus E. Dallin 1861-1944, Springville. Sculptor

Laraine Day b. 1917, Roosevelt. Film actress: *The Locket, The Third Voice*

Bernard De Voto 1897-1955, Ogden. Pulitzer Prize-winning historian

Kelly Downs b. 1960, Ogden. Baseball pitcher

Marriner S. Eccles 1890-1977, Logan. Financier

Philo T. Farnsworth 1906-71, Beaver. Inventor of electronic devices that led to the invention of television

Maude Adams reached the height of her career in 1905 as the lead in the play Peter Pan.

Bernard De Voto received a Pulitzer Prize in 1947 for his book Across the Wide Mississippi.

Herman Franks b. 1914, Price. Baseball manager

Gene Fullmer b. 1931, West Jordan. Middleweight boxing champion

John Gilbert 1895-1936, Logan. Silent film actor: *Love, Queen Christina*

William D. Haywood 1869-1928, Salt Lake City. Labor organizer

John Held, Jr. 1889-1958, Salt Lake City. Cartoonist and

David McKay was the ninth president (1951-70) of the Mormon church. The membership in the church increased from 1.1 to 2.9 million in the 19 years of McKay's leadership.

illustrator

Frank T. Hines 1879-1960, Salt Lake City. Army officer and government official

Bruce Hurst b. 1958, St. George. Baseball pitcher

Florence P. Kahn 1866-1948, Salt Lake City. Congresswoman

Goodwin J. Knight 1896-1970, Provo. Governor of California

David O. McKay 1873-1970, Huntsville. President of the Church of Jesus Christ of Latter-Day Saints

Dick Motta b. 1931, Salt Lake City. Professional basketball coach

Red Nichols 1905-65, Ogden. Jazz trumpeter and bandleader

Merlin Olsen b. 1940, Logan. Hall of Fame football player

Donny Osmond b. 1957, Ogden. Pop singer

Marie Osmond b. 1959, Ogden. Pop singer

Ivy Baker Priest 1905-75, Kimberley. U.S. Treasurer

Dick Romney 1895-1969, Salt Lake City. College football coach

Byron Scott b. 1961, Ogden. Basketball player

George Albert Smith 1870-1951, Salt Lake City. President of the Church of Jesus Christ of Latter-day Saints

Reed O. Smoot 1862-1941, Salt Lake City. Senate leader

Virginia Sorensen 1912-91, Provo. Novelist: *A Little Lower than the Angels; The Neighbors*

Elbert D. Thomas 1883-1953, Salt Lake City. Senate leader

Robert Walker 1914-51, Salt Lake City. Film actor: *One Touch of Venus, Strangers on a Train*

Ervin Wardman 1865-1923, Salt Lake City. Journalist

Loretta Young b. 1913, Salt Lake City. Academy Award-winning actress: *The Farmer's Daughter, Come to the Stable*

Mahonri M. Young 1877-1957, Salt Lake City. Sculptor

Colleges and Universities

There are several colleges and universities in Utah. Here are the more prominent, with their locations, dates of founding, and enrollments.

Brigham Young University, Provo, 1875, 28,282

Southern Utah State College, Cedar City, 1897, 4,411

University of Utah, Salt Lake City, 1850, 19,816

Utah State University, Logan, 1888, 12,854

Weber State College, Ogden, 1889, 14,837

Westminster College of Salt Lake City, Salt Lake City, 1875, 1,711

Where To Get More Information

Utah Travel Council
Council Hall
Capitol Hill
Salt Lake City UT 84114
Or call 1-801-538-1030

Philo T. Farnsworth (1907-1971), who invented the early television receiver, was born in Beaver, Utah.

Further Reading

General

Aylesworth, Thomas G. and Virginia L. Aylesworth. *State Reports: The West: Arizona, Nevada & Utah.* New York: Chelsea House, 1992.

Arizona

Arizona, A Guide to the Grand Canyon State. New York: Hastings House, 1940.

Baker, Betty. *States of the Nation: Arizona.* New York: Coward-McCann, 1969.

Carpenter, Allan. *Arizona,* rev. ed. Chicago: Childrens Press, 1979.

Chanin, Abe and Mildred Chanin. *This Land, These Voices: A Different View of Arizona History in the Words of Those Who Lived It.* Flagstaff, AZ: Northland Press, 1977.

Heinrichs, Ann. *America the Beautiful: Arizona.* Chicago: Childrens Press, 1991.

Love, Frank. *Arizona's Story: A Short History.* New York: Norton, 1979.

Miller, Joseph. *Arizona; The Grand Canyon State; A State Guide,* rev. ed. New York: Hastings House, 1966.

Powell, Lawrence Clark. *Arizona: A Bicentennial History.* New York: Norton, 1977.

Trimble, Marshall. *Arizona: A Panoramic History of a Frontier State.* Garden City, NY: Doubleday, 1977.

Nevada

Angel, Myron, ed. *History of Nevada.* New York: Arno Press, 1973.

Carpenter, Allan. *Nevada,* rev. ed. Chicago: Childrens Press, 1979.

Elliott, Russell R. *History of Nevada.* Lincoln, NE: University of Nebraska Press, 1973.

Fradin, Dennis B. *Nevada in Words and Pictures.* Chicago: Childrens Press, 1981.

Hulse, James W. *The Nevada Adventure: A History,* 5th ed. Reno, NV: University of Nevada Press, 1981.

Laxalt, Robert. *Nevada: A Bicentennial History.* New York: Norton, 1977.

Lillard, Richard G. *Desert Challenge: An Interpretation of Nevada.* Westport, CT: Greenwood, 1979.

Lillegard, Dee, and Wayne Stoker. *America the Beautiful: Nevada.* Chicago: Childrens Press, 1991.

Utah

Carpenter, Allan. *Utah,* rev. ed. Chicago: Childrens Press, 1979.

Fradin, Dennis B. *Utah in Words and Pictures.* Chicago: Childrens Press, 1980.

Luce, Willard and Celia Luce. *Utah!* Layton, UT: Peregrine Smith, 1975.

McCarthy, Betty. *America the Beautiful: Utah.* Chicago: Childrens Press, 1990.

Peterson, Charles S. *Utah, A History.* New York: Norton, 1984.

Poll, Richard D., and others, eds. *Utah's History.* Provo, UT: Brigham Young University Press, 1978.

Numbers in italics refer to illustrations

Picture Credits

Courtesy of Arizona Office of Tourism: pp. 3 (top), 7, 8-9, 10, 11, 12, 14, 15, 16, 17, 18, 19, 20, 21, 22, 23, 24, 25, 26-27, 29, 30, 33, 34; Courtesy of Arizona Secretary of State: p. 5; Courtesy of Church of Jesus Christ of Latter-Day Saints: p. 92; Courtesy of City of Phoenix Public Information Office/Bob Rink: p. 13; Culver: pp. 32, 81; Frank Jensen: p. 63; Library of Congress: pp. 80, 85; Jim Maire: p. 79; Hughes Martin: pp. 64-65; Courtesy of National Park Service/Margaret Farrell: p. 71; National Portrait Gallery: p. 54; Courtesy of Nevada Commission on Tourism: pp. 3 (bottom), 37, 38, 40-41, 42, 44, 45, 46, 47, 48, 49, 50, 52, 53, 55, 57, 58; Courtesy of *Nevada Magazine*/Caroline Joy Hadley: pp. 43, 51; Courtesy of Office of Morris Udall: p. 36; Courtesy of Park City Chamber/Bureau: pp. 74, 75; Courtesy of Salt Lake Convention and Visitors Bureau: pp. 66, 68, 69, 70, 72, 73, 90; Courtesy of Utah Historical Society: p. 91; Courtesy of Utah Travel Council: pp. 61, 65, 76, 77, 78, 83, 88-89; Courtesy of Utah Travel Council/Scott T. Smith: p. 67; Wide World: pp. 35, 59, 86, 93.

Cover photos courtesy of Arizona Office of Tourism; Salt Lake Convention and Visitors Bureau; and Nevada Commission on Tourism.